101
Uses
for a
Horse

101
Uses
for a
Horse

Willow Creek Press
Minocqua, Wisconsin

101 Uses for a Horse
Edited by Melissa Sovey-Nelson

© 2003 Willow Creek Press

Published by Willow Creek Press
P.O. Box 147 • Minocqua, Wisconsin 54548

Design: Andrea Donner

Printed in Canada

Willow Creek®
P R E S S

Horses as

. . . as

faithful

companions

1 *Yoga partner*

© Dusty L. Perin

2 *Cot*

3

Someone to laugh at your jokes

© Dusty L. Perin

4 *Matchmaker*

© Alan & Sandy Carey

5 *Someone to relax with...*

© Dusty L. Perin

6

...and to share a drink with

© Dusty L. Perin

7 *Teammate*

© Bob Langrish

8
Classmate

© Bob Langrish

9 *Campmate*

11
Babysitter

Mountain to climb

© Alan & Sandy Carey

13

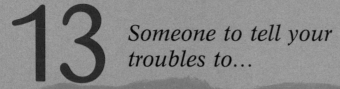

 *Someone to tell your
troubles to...*

© Lynn M. Stone

14

*...who
will really
listen*

© Lynn M. Stone

15

Someone to soar with

© Chris Harvey / Ardea.com

16 *Someone to bathe with*

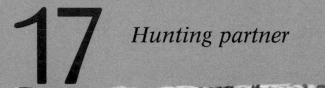

17 *Hunting partner*

© Bob Langrish

18 *Workout partner*

© Lynn M. Stone

19

Someone
to set...

© Bob Langrish

20

...and achieve goals with

© Bob Langrish

21 *Builder of self-esteem…*

© DenverBryan.com

22

...and courage

© DenverBryan.com

23

Someone to make you a stable person

© DenverBryan.com

24
Best friend

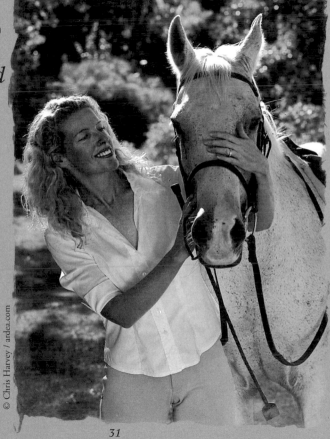

25

Someone to grow up with...

© Dusty L. Perin

26 *...and to grow old with*

© DenverBryan.com

. . . as

tireless

workers

27 *Logger*

© Bob Langrish

28 *Lawn mowers*

© DenverBryan.com

29
Trail blazer

© Bob Langrish

30 *Taxi*

Bus driver

© Bob Langrish

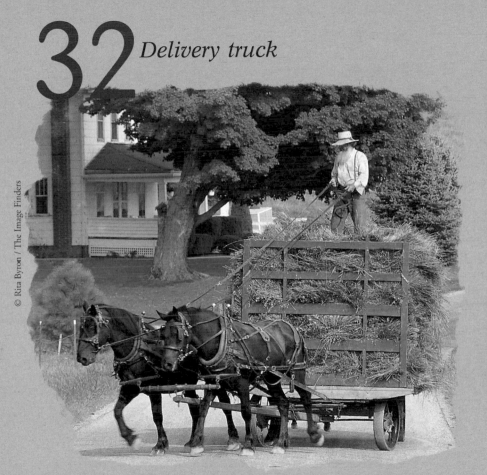

© Bob Langrish

34

Police officer

© Bob Langrish

35 *Farmhand*

© Lynn M. Stone

36 *Chauffeur*

37 *Competitor*

© Alice Garik / Peter Arnold, Inc.

38 *Crowd control*

© M. Watson / Ardea.com

39 *Mountain guide*

40 *Tour guide*

41

Gardener

© M. Watson / Ardea.com

42
Valet

© Bob Langrish

43 *Mail carrier*

© Londie G. Padelsky

44 *Athlete*

© Bob Langrish

45 *Someone to help make maple sugar*

© Lynn M. Stone

46

Circus performer

© Bob Langrish

47

Turn signal

48 *Team player*

© Terry Wild Studio, Inc.

© Bob Langrish

. . . and
specialty
uses

49

Head rest

50

*Window
dressing*

© Johan De Meester / Ardea.com

51 *Family sedan*

© Terry Wild Studio, Inc.

52

Lawn ornaments

© Terry Wild Studio, Inc.

53 *Beach comber*

© Bob Langrish

54 *Gatekeeper*

© Lynn M. Stone

55 *Alarm bell*

© Lynn M. Stone

56 Soccer player

© Dusty L. Perin

57 *Dog trainer*

58 *Dog walker*

© Alan & Sandy Carey

59

Cat sitter

© Renee Stockdale / AnimalsAnimals

60

Calm in a storm

© Terry Wild Studio, Inc.

Someone to help you find your center

62

*Wordless
communicator*

63

Ego booster

© Dusty L. Perin

Someone to answer the door

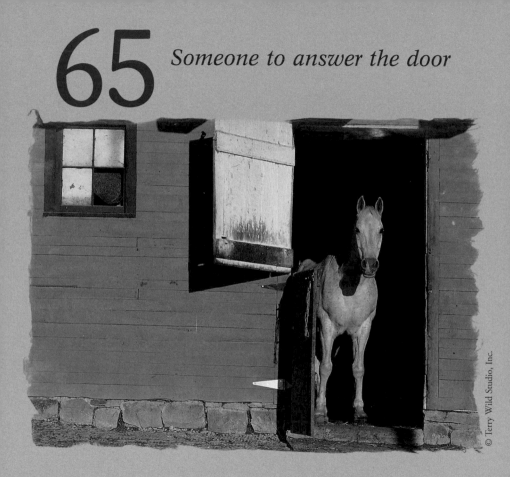

66
Lookout

© Bob Langrish

67

Someone to bring out your maternal instincts

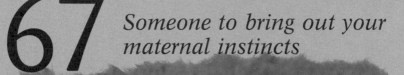

© Dusty L. Perin

68

Someone to share your pride with

© Dusty L. Perin

79

© Londie G. Padelsky

70 *Snowmobile*

© Helmut Gritscher / Peter Arnold, Inc.

71 *Snow angel*

© Bob Langrish

72
Snowshoes

© Alan & Sandy Carey

Ceremonial leader

© Bob Langrish

*Partner in
defeat…*

© Bob Langrish

76

...and in triumph

© Bob Langrish

77
Dandelion control

Photographer's assistant

© B&C Beck

79 *Bookends*

80 *Someone to stand up for you*

© Bob Langrish

81

*Role
model*

82
Supermodel

© Bob Langrish

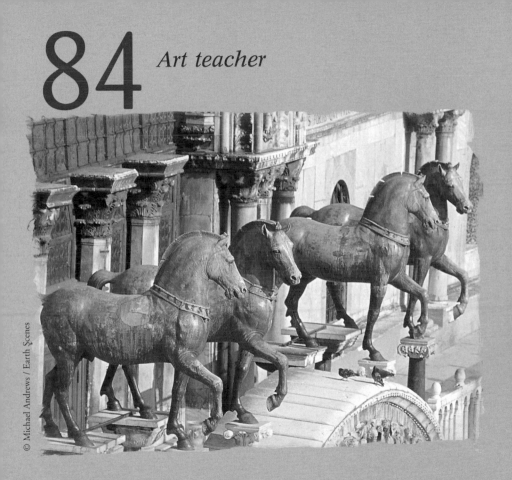

85 *Entertainer*

© Alan & Sandy Carey

86 *Telephone booth*

© Alan & Sandy Carey

87

*Honest
commentator*

© Zig Leszczynski / AnimalsAnimals

© Dusty L. Perin

© Bob Langrish

© Renee Stockdale / AnimalsAnimals

92

*Floral
arranger*

93
Motivator

© Londie G. Padelsky

94

*Someone
to make
you reflect*

© Wendy Shattil / Bob Rozinski

95

*Someone to enrich
your horizons*

© Londie G. Padelsky

96

Someone
to bring
you roses

© Sharon Eide / Elizabeth Flynn

97

Fly swatter

© DusanSmetana.com

Childhood memory

© Londie G. Padelsky

99

Someone to start...

© Wendy Shattil / Bob Rozinski

100 *... and end your day with*